How to Use

Your Power

of Visualization

How to Use Your Power of Visualization

by Emily Bradley Lyons

PUBLISHED BY LYONS VISUALIZATION SERIES

For information address Emily Bradley Lyons,
Lyons Visualization Series,
19065 Saint Croy Road, Red Bluff, California 96080.

ISBN: 0-960-4374-0-1

Published by Lyons Visualization Series
First printing April 1980
Second printing September 1987

Design & illustration: Bonnie Jean Smetts

Typesetting: Golden Rule Printing
                           Willits, California

Printing: Walker Lithograph, Inc.
                           Red Bluff, California

Additional typesetting: Accent & Alphabet
                           Berkeley, California

                           Solotype
                           Oakland, California

                           Richard Ellington
                           Oakland, California

                           Walker Lithograph, Inc.
                           Red Bluff, California

DEDICATION

To: Vannie
          Skeff
          Alex

Who — from the Far Country —
continue to teach us
that the Power of
Visualization
lies within ourselves —
in the silence beyond
word and thought —

Contents

Foreword
by G.N. Getman, O.D.

As one enters the Childrens' Museum in Washington, D.C., a large
and very visible poster is immediately sighted and both its design
and message demand attention. It says:

> "Hear ..... and forget."
> "See ...... and remember."
> "Do .... and understand."

The last two phrases are most appropriate to this book you are
about to read. If all you do is "see" it you will still remember it
for several reasons. It is a delightful discussion of a human ability
to which neither scientist nor educator has given enough attention.
You will also remember it because it is not a book for casual reading, but neither is it a heavy and overwhelming book. It is a book
for anyone who desires to reach for and grasp some of the poten-
tials that slumber within each of us.

The last phrase of the museum poster is even more relevant to
this book. If all you do is read it, and neglect to take the opportunity it offers to participate . . . to "do" . . . you will miss the full
awareness and appreciation of your inherent information systems,
and all the knowledge that is availailable to you in the world and
cultures in which you live. Doing exactly what the book suggests,
in the well detailed procedures that are easy to follow, will let you,
and every other reader and participator, learn how to control and

organize all the information that surrounds us to your benefit instead of the usual attempts to cope with or ignore our confusions. All of the benefits can become available through the information system which is most prominent in all human behavior . . . the visual system. One only need to follow the clearly outlined instructions given here to discover what primary experience really is, and just how quickly and effectively attitudes can be changed to find the joys and beauties of a more sensitive and vital self.

Although the emphasis of this book is upon the visual system, and its unique ability to extend and expand visual thinking, one will find other systems becoming much more available and alert in responsiveness. It is a great experience for one to arrive at the realization that there are a myriad of appreciations one can explore and expand through this visualization process so well detailed here. A fuller recognition of the interpersonal relationships and the wealth of these is one new realm. Another new realm can be the recognition of the values of melody and rhythm that can make each day move more smoothly. Still another is the awareness of the importance and the worth of a world full of textures that comes as one achieves a deeper feeling for the ever-constant surroundings. And, for a climax, there can be an internal glow of growing self-esteem and peace as one more fully discovers how exciting the world can be, and what one's place in it can really be.

This will be an important book. It will have great influence upon parents, teachers, developmental optometrists, other thoughtful clinicians and all of those for whom it has been written. The author has not only put much of herself into this book; she has also included the lives and the developments of literally hundreds of children and adults whom she has assisted to a more fulfilling life. The messages in this book come from a long and insightful first-hand experience of working with people who needed to see and know the world better than they were able to by themselves.

One of those to whom Emily Lyons has dedicated this book kept reminding us: "We teach a child nothing . . . we can only arrange the conditions in which a child can learn." This book is a splendid example of the arranging of conditions for the benefit of every reader who participates in its recommendations. Do not rush through this book. Do not lay it down until you have a bit more time. Do not fail to give it every consideration and exploration. You will only be cheating yourself if you do any of these.

G. N. Getman, O.D., D.O.S.

Acknowledgements

It is difficult to evaluate the depth of influence that individual persons have had on my thinking, or to assess what part their love and support has contributed to my creativity. To list all would form a separate volume in itself, but, special mention must be given to a few:

Jane Brown — my teacher and friend who, through dance has taught me the principles of effortless movement, opening new vistas of visualization.

Herbert and Betty Fitch — whose spiritual guidance and Infinite Way seminars have contributed so profoundly to opening new Views for me.

Golden Rule Publications and Printing — and my deep gratitude especially to: Lloyd and Mae Connerly — for years of faith in this work, and for the broad understanding to bring it to publication.

Robert Barnes Monroe — my husband and best friend whose love makes it all worthwhile.

xi

I owe much to all of the optometrists throughout the country who have participated in my seminar-workshops and have contributed so much to my thinking. I am especially indebted to the Optometric Extension Program Foundation, and the role it has played in my life. Without the functional thinking of this group, which was so excellently and wisely interpreted by my late husband, C. Venard Lyons, O. D., who shared this wisdom with me, this book would never have been written. I wish to particularly mention, with gratitude, a few of my optometrist friends who have given me enduring and dedicated friendship:

Caryl Croisant, Tole Greenstein, Gerald Getman, Donald Getz, Homer Hendrickson, Wayne Musser, Ralph Schrock, Amorita Treganza, Bruce Wolff.

Also, my thanks to the optometric vision therapists and assistants throughout the country, who have welcomed me in their groups by sharing and participating.

To my special family, "the Potters"— Ginny, Bud, Kim, Kris, and Ken (who allowed us to adopt him), I give gratitude and love for influencing my thinking by bringing joy in so many ways.

To Carlene Schnabel for sharing her expertise in ways and means of publishing a book.

To Bonnie Smetts for the thought, love and dedication that has gone into the design and illustrations. To comment on their excellence seems redundant, as they so obviously speak for themselves.

And finally to my students, of all ages, who have taught me far more than I have taught them. I especially wish to thank a few who have given me warm and enduring friendship, who have understood and applied the principles of visualization more than most:

Dinah and Charlotte Dethero, Cheryl Hallett, Miriam Lawler, Bonnie Smetts, Scott Smith, Joe Watson.

Who Can Use This Book

This book is not designed for a specific field or age. The visual principles presented apply to all ages and levels of thinking. Since they are principles not limited to visual improvement only, but are universal principles that can be applied to daily living, new viewpoints and new horizons open. Working with these principles is working with oneself as a total person.

This is a personal book, meant to be used by the reader for finding a new view of him/herself, or through the teacher (therapist, counselor, parent) for their students/children to find new dimensions in their visual world.

It is a book that can be used in many ways by many people. Some suggested uses might be:

BY—

- Visual Do-It-Yourselfers of all ages
- Optometrists and vision therapists, who, more than most professions, should understand and use visualization as part of their visual therapy and vision training.
- Parents, for themselves and for their children to guide the development of their visual memory and visual thinking.
- Counselors, to assist people to find visual direction, bringing a new view of living.
- Camp directors, with youngsters by the campfire, or lakeside.

- Dance teachers and therapists, to enhance visual direction and dimension in their students.
- Movement and awareness instructors, to realize the relationship between movement and vision.
- All teachers, to improve, not only their own visual imagery and memory, but, also, that of their students. Surprisingly, they may discover an added benefit of improved reading skill.

Viewpoint and Intent

The intent of this book is to help you expand your visual awareness and visual consciousness. The purpose of the Visualization Views is to awaken unsuspected dimension within yourself through contact with your outer and inner visual worlds.

This book is designed for all who have realized, either consciously or sub-consciously, the significance of visual imagery, visual thinking, and visualization in their lives. Some may have phrased this realization as a question such as, "How do I learn to visualize?" Others may have acquired the skill of visually picturing, may believe they understand visualization, but are unable to make these abilities part of their daily living. Still others may have found their thoughts, their mental imagery and reading moving in slow gear, reduced to the rate and incessant chatter of their tyrannical inner verbalizer.

Whoever and wherever you are on the path, this is a book for all seekers in the quest of that dynamic, silent, visual process, known by many names — and yet beyond all words and thoughts — for which we are using the words, "visualization."

Visualization has been used as a catch-all word to cover a bewildering array of meanings. For this reason, and to help clarify thinking, in this book a differentiation is made between the terms, "Visualizing", "Visual Thinking", and "Visualization."

To Visualize (or Visualizing) is involvement in conscious visual imagery, or picturing. In the visualizing, or visual imagery stage, picturing is usually supported by other senses — namely verbal.

Visual Thinking is visualizing, or visual picturing, released from verbal (or other sensory involvement).

Visualization is difficult to pin down to any single definition, but, as nearly as it can be confined, we might say that it is the "knowing", dynamic, silent, effortless, visual state released from the prison of time and space.

The roots of visualization rest deeply in visual picturing, or visual imagery, aided and reinforced by one or more supporting sense. As we learn and refine visual principles, becoming less dependent on the support of other senses, visual picturing tends to emerge free from involvement with other senses. The most persistent visual companion is inner speech, that little prompting verbalizer that accompanies much of our visual imagery. However, as this, too, becomes unnecessary, visual picturing emerges released from the verbal prompter. As we continue the journey, eventually, a state is reached where even visual picturing is sublimated.

The process progresses in stages of discarding earlier states of learning that are no longer needed. As the worm goes into the cocoon for a period of silence, to emerge as the butterfly, so emerges a different process known as visualization. And yet, even in this greatest visual refinement, dimly retained are the very definitely learned abilities, the concrete matching between all sensory systems, the solid base that allows us to soar.

These are the visual principles and stages of learning presented in the Visualization View of the workbook.

Organization and Use

Organization

The Applied Visualization Workbook is divided into five major headings, or Views. Each View forms one aspect of the visualization process, with three sub-headings (or three weeks of work) elaborating the aspects of that View.

Each week is divided into six days of projects, with an introduction page discussing the thinking emphasized for that week.

The six days of projects are presented so they may be studied, visualized, worked with, then recorded in writing.

A review week is given at the end of View III, reviewing the nine weeks of work, before proceeding to Views IV, and V, bringing a total of sixteen weeks of study.

Use

The general format of the book is designed for an individual to use with him/herself on a daily basis. Adaptations to this may be made by instructors or parents working with their students or children. However, because the principles developed are organized sequentially from elementary to more complex skills of visualization, it is suggested that the order be maintained as given, to develop the skills and thinking for each day and each week. As you tackle the projects, one-a-day as suggested, you gain greater insight into the visualization process. It is a cumulative process, from View to View, which suffers if any step is deleted or skipped. Each View contributes to the greater whole.

The importance of writing the learning of each day cannot be over-emphasized. A journal type of recording should be continued throughout the days and weeks of work. Much learning comes from reviewing these observations to ourselves. By writing experiences in detail we develop a capacity for observation and ease in communication. Verbal and written modes of thinking and communication are complimentary. They expand our viewpoint and save us from falling into the "language rut", or a limited, one-way of expressing ourselves.

You can write to yourself, or to another person, or you and another (or a number of persons) can study the Views together, then write to one another about them. You may use these study sessions to share your experiences.

Do not skip days or leave blanks. Ask yourself, "Why am I having difficulty with this?" Discussing why it is difficult to write your thoughts may bring insight into parts of yourself you have ignored or avoided.

Applied Visualization

The Views

Orchestration of the Senses

WEEK ONE
The Orchestra

WEEK TWO
The Concert Master
Visual Principles for Living

WEEK THREE
Combining Orchestra
and Concert Master
Living This Moment

Week One   The Orchestra

Vision is a mirror of what you have learned through all of your senses: taste, touch, smell, feeling, hearing-speaking. If there are holes or hollows in the learning through these senses, there will be matching holes or hollows in the learning through your vision. Wherever limitations exist, you will find the same limitations existing in what you "see" and understand, because you "see" only what you know and have learned with your total body.

When vision is limited and restricted, visual imagery will be equally limited, because the images in your mind evolve out of the orchestration of your senses. Visualization, the ultimate visual process, is the theme, the celestial music that emerges when your orchestra blends into one great whole unit.

In order to find what each sensory musician is contributing to your orchestra, during this week you will check in with each one to find out how much you are noticing or ignoring. You will study each member of the orchestra except vision, which will be your study for next week.

Each day during this week observe and write down what you have learned about each one of your senses:

During this day discover something new about something that you have tasted many times. What have you ignored about it? Study the texture, qualities of sweet, sour, salty, bitter, moisture, dryness. Is there a lingering after taste? Is it different from how it tasted before? Also during this day, taste something that you would not taste before. Discover why it is repugnant, or why you have avoided it before. Analyze it in the same way that you did with the familiar taste.

Day 1

TASTE
(Gustatory)

Discover some new quality of odor in something very familiar to you. Smell it as if you were smelling it for the first time. Does anything about it surprise you? Also, on this day, smell something that you would not usually smell. Smell many different things such as: a rock, a piece of metal, a piece of cloth. Find an odor in everything around you.

Day 2

SMELL
(Olfactory)

Day 3

TOUCH
(Tactile)

Touch something very familiar and discover something new about it that you had not noticed before. Let your fingers really get acquainted with it. What do they discover that they have not noticed before? Also, during this day, touch something that you have either avoided touching, or that you have not thought of touching. What did you discover about it that surprised you?

Day 4

MOVEMENT
(Kinesthesia)

Study your own movements that you know very well. What do you discover about them? How does your walk feel to you? Does it feel graceful and light, or does it feel heavy and awkward? Are your movements inclined to be propulsive and headlong, or are they slow and precise? Do you feel you usually move efficiently and well? Also, on this day, try moving in a different way, walk a new way, dance a new dance. In other words, try a movement you had not tried before.

Listen to something that is a familiar part of your life. Hear something in the sound that you had not noticed before, such as quality of highness, lowness, sharpness, delicacy, soothing, pleasing, irritating. What surprised you about the sound as you analyzed it this way? Also, during this day, hear a sound that you had either not noticed before, or had not heard before. Extend your range of highs and lows. Find out what you ignore in sounds around you.

Day 5
HEARING
(Audition)

Use your own voice in a new or different way. If you usually speak slowly, try speaking very rapidly. If you speak rapidly, obviously slow it down. What do you notice about your own voice that you had not noticed before? Notice how the sounds of words are made with your mouth. What surprises you about any of this? Also, this day, sing! Even if you feel you can't sing a note, still sing. What do you discover about it?

Day 6
SPEECH
(Verbal)

Each day write down your observations. Write in detail so that you will have a picture of your visualizations. It is important that you *write* your observations. Written expression is an essential part of the ability to visually concentrate. Most persons drop easily into verbal description, but avoid written expression. This is your opportunity to discover your ignored or blunted inner sensory resources, and how to accomplish a balanced orchestration of those senses.

This is the base for full, vivid mental imagery and imagination. Incidentally, it has a rather valuable fringe benefit of producing more alert mental functioning.

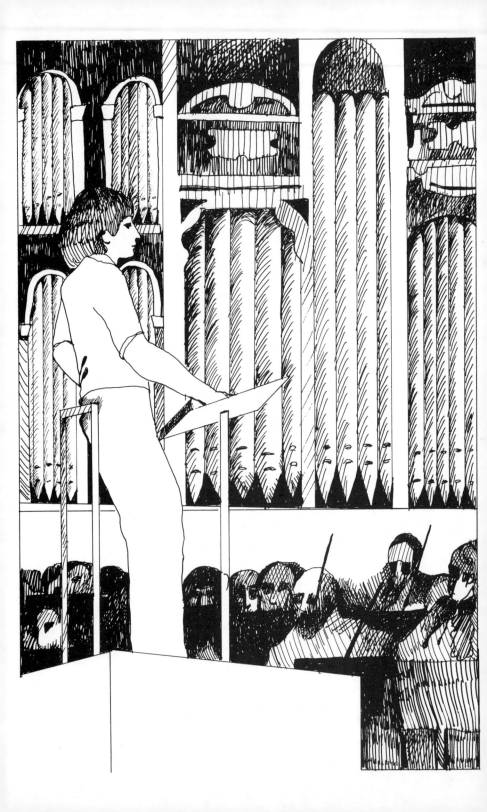

The Concert Master

Visual Principles for Living

You have been learning about your orchestra and discovering the quality of music it produces. Also, perhaps you are discovering that some sections of your orchestra are not contributing as fully as they could. As you attend to these musicians, practicing with them, and encouraging each one of them, they can make a greater contribution to the harmonic wholeness of the symphony.

During this week you will be working with the concert master of your symphony, your visual imagery. In the same way that a concert master brings all the discrete parts of the orchestra into a blended whole preparing for the conductor, so visual imagery weaves the senses into a unit for

Vision, the conductor, to use as an instrument for creating the magnificent music of visualization.

In preparation, you will study some of the basic processes and principles necessary for developing the full, rich imaging part of visualization. Each day during this week you will work with a different principle. Each day, observe and write down what you have learned that day.

During this day concentrate on programming yourself with visual images rather than instructing yourself with words. Learn to watch, and learn by watching. Don't analyze; simply observe. Find some activity that, ordinarily, you do not do well. Before you do it, give yourself a clear, visual image of how you want to do it. Allow yourself to watch yourself very closely. Repeat the process and *feel* what it is like to do the activity as you mentally picture yourself doing it. After you have pictured, and felt the activity, do it. Observe what happened — don't analyze — just find how well you continued to visualize and feel. Watch with detachment, as if you are watching someone else. Feel no concern about anything except that you are continuing visualizing and matching your feeling with your visualizing.

Day 1

See Don't Say

On this day you have three projects to work with and apply this principle:

Project 1 — Listen to one person without bringing in your judgment of what the person is saying. Wait until the person is completely finished speaking. Really listen without deciding if you agree or disagree; just hear what the person has to say. Did you find yourself listening with greater concentration without your mind wandering to your own inner verbalizing?

Project 2 — Look at something with which you are very familiar, something that you have seen many times before. Look at it as

Day 2

Let Go of Judicial Judgement

if you had never seen it before. Look at it as you were looking through the eyes of another person. Do not judge it good or bad; simply see it.

Project 3 — Read something, preferably a short article. As you read, try not to decide if the article is good or bad, right or wrong, but hear what the author has to say. Make no judgment until you have finished the article. Do you notice you recall more than you ordinarily would have? What else did you notice?

Day 3

Trust Your Visualizing and Don't Argue with It

During this day practice trusting yourself. Concentrate on not letting yourself talk yourself out of doing things. Do something where, ordinarily, you would give yourself a series of self-instructions. Visualize what you want to do, then *let* yourself do it without *making* yourself do it. Take one thing where, ordinarily, you would say, "I *must* do this", and think, "I *want* to do this." Stop trying too hard all day; just allow things to happen.

How was the day — easier?

During this day, combine and work with all of the projects of Days 1, 2, and 3. Write any observations that are different from the first days.

Day 4

Repeat Day 4; again writing any new observations.

Day 5

Review your written work to make certain you have recorded all of your thinking, then relax and enjoy the results of your visualizing.

Day 6

Week Three

Combining Orchestra and Concert Master

Living This Moment

Now that you are becoming better acquainted with all of your senses, you can learn how much they are willing to bring to you if only you will move out of their way and *allow* them to help you.

Last week you learned that, as you practiced the three important principles of: trusting your visualizing; releasing from judging while creatively thinking; and looking without verbally labeling, you encouraged your creative visualizing to release and open up more of the world around. You also may be discovering that this new awareness is bringing you greater concentration, as your mind remains in the here-and-now moment, rather than jumping from past to future, as a hummingbird zooms from blossom to blossom.

Your project this week is continuing and extending this ability to remain in the present moment as you concentrate on what is occurring in that moment. Each day observe and write down what you have learned that day.

Each day choose a time when you will have ten uninterrupted minutes where you can concentrate on this project. It may be anyplace: inside, outside, while waiting for an appointment — wherever you have ten minutes. Always have a notebook and pencil handy. Time yourself. During those ten minutes write down as much as you can write.

In order to remind your humming-bird mind that it is this moment that you are writing about, and not some tomorrow or yesterday, begin each sentence with words that define the present, such as one of these: now, here, at this moment, at this instant, at this time, etc.

As an example, you might write, "Now, sitting here on this chair, as I write, I can feel the edge of the chair on my legs. At this moment, the light from the lamp shines on the page and I am aware of the reflection. At this instant, I hear the waves on the beach as the wind blows the water. At this time, I discover the inside of my mouth feels dry. Now, I feel an itch on my arm and I scratch it. Now I smell food cooking in the kitchen — etc." By describing the scene and situation you are in, as given in the example, you engage your mind in the present moment.

Days 4, 5 and 6

Review what you have written on the first three days. Analyze and make the following observations:

1. Did you remain in the present, or did you, without realizing it, wander into future or past happenings?

2. Were you more aware of certain sensory processes to the exclusion of others?

3. Were your observations all directed externally to yourself, or were you also aware of what was going on internally in your own body?

Now work with Days 4-5-6, filling in any omissions in any of the above three areas.

As you continue to add to the richness of your visual imagery throughout every day (not only this one week), you will find increased ability to concentrate at each moment wherever you are.

Inner Visual Centering

WEEK FOUR
Island of Tranquility
and Screen of the Mind

WEEK FIVE
Visualizing Light

WEEK SIX
Finding Order in Chaos
Central – Peripheral

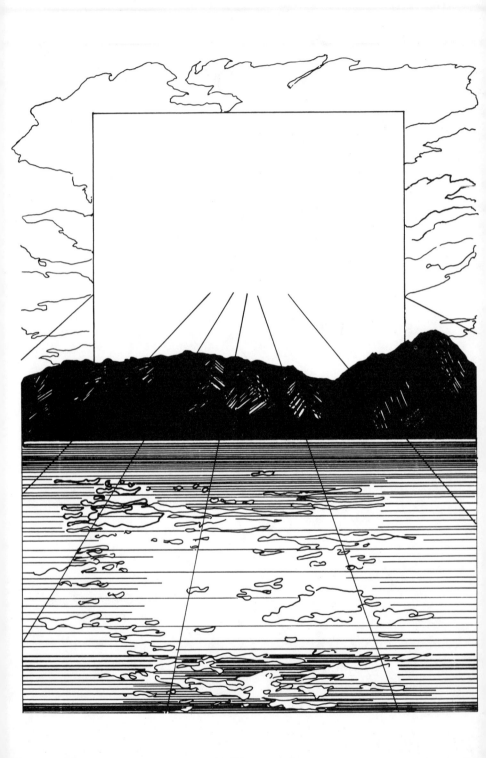

Week Four

Island of Tranquility and Screen of the Mind

As you learn to be more visually aware of each moment, you will find a quiet and stillness where-ever you are, even in the so-called turmoil of life, under the most trying and difficult conditions.

Within this great visual activity there exists a silence and stillness like the poise of a humming-bird's wings, or the center of a spinning top. You can rest into it and enjoy it undisturbed, as you tune yourself to the differences in rhythms that exist inside and outside of yourself.

This week you will continue learning to still your mind and find your own inner center, as you deepen and extend your visualization ability. This will be a project of concentration in visual imagery. During the entire process, attempt to keep yourself in a relaxed state of visual picturing.

Day 1

First: Find a place where you can be alone for about fifteen minutes. Second: Carefully read over the instructions so you will visually recall the entire sequence without re-reading.

Instructions: Settle yourself comfortably and close your eyes. Your eyes will be closed during the entire project.

With your eyes closed, take a deep breath and exhale. Then direct your attention to your eyelids, in particular the little muscles around your eyes. Relax these muscles and let them go. Feel this relaxation move like a wave slowly downward throughout your entire body. Continue to breathe slowly and deeply. Each time that you breathe out, feel yourself becoming more and more relaxed. Allow your body to rest as you breathe in and out and relax.

This should allow you to reach a deeper and more inward visual level of mind. To help you tune in more fully to your inner levels of mind, choose a passive scene from nature, or any scene that you find serenely beautiful and tranquil. It should be a place in which you feel strong, happy and at ease, a place where you feel as excellent as you ever have. Visualize and put yourself within that place, for this will be your own special Island of Tranquility. Reach out and feel the vibrant life forces that surround you, and feel in perfect tune with your inner visual levels of mind. Put aside all conscious intellectualizing and thinking; let your imagination roam over this scene.

As you continue relaxing into your subconscious visual levels, you will project out into space in front of you, the numbers from twelve down to one. You are not to verbalize the numbers, but to see them appear and disappear in order. On each descending number, feel yourself becoming more and more relaxed, nearer to the source of your visual thinking. When you reach the number one, you should experience a feeling of great relaxation and rest, with your mind released from its usual verbalizing and intellectualizing. Rest there for a moment.

Next, visually create a screen in the space in front of you. It may be as far away, or as near to you as you wish. Make the screen as large, or as small as you wish. Design it to your own tastes, for this will be your own Screen of the Mind's Eye. In the future, any problems that you wish to solve, or conditions you wish to change, will be projected onto your Screen of Mind.

Next, project onto your screen a condition that you would like to change. Picture this condition very clearly, with all its problems. Then erase the condition completely, and project onto your screen the changed condition that you wish. Visualize it vividly in complete detail. When you have pictured it to your satisfaciton, you will speak these words to your subconscious mind, "Erase all of those negative thoughts and pictures that you have been holding and accept no record from them. You will hold the truth as I am picturing it here and now." Then open your eyes feeling rested and revitalized, with a wider and fuller visual understanding of yourself and the world around you.

Now that you have read and visualized the

instructions, close your eyes and use your visual imagery to picture the sequence and to apply it.

When you have completed the sequence, re-read the instructions to find if you visualized completely.

Days 2, 3, 4, 5 and 6

Each day repeat Day 1. You may use the same condition or problem, or you may choose a different one. Adapt it to your own use.

Your written work:

Day 1 — Write your experiences. Did you clearly visualize the sequence?

Day 2 — Write your experiences and anything new you discovered.

Day 3 — Write your experiences and if you are relaxing easier and quicker.

Day 4 — Write your experiences. Is your visual imagery becoming more vivid?

Day 5 — Write your experiences. Do not write, "just like before", but do write your pictures vividly and visually.

Day 6 — This should be a sum-up of what you feel you are learning from this project.

Week Five

Visualizing Light

You are continuing your study of learning to still your mind and to find your own inner visual center.

This week you will work with an activity that can be used anytime when you find that you and your world around is not as vital, vibrant and bright as it might be.

It is easy to forget, in the press of active, busy days, that sunlight is our greatest source of energy. It is also easy to forget that vision is the result of the use of light-related energy, and that visualization ability is dependent on how well we are able to use light.

Research in many fields is proving the need of full-spectrum sunlight passing through the eyes, so the importance of daily sunlight in the eyes cannot be over-emphasized. If we neglect this significant concept, our visual and bodily well-being will be directly reduced in proportion to the amount of light we experience, and how well we circulate that energy through our bodies.

This activity will give you practice in learning to visualize light moving throughout your entire body.

Repeat View II, Week 4, Day 1, Instructions through the countdown of twelve to one, to the paragraph that says, "Rest there for a moment." Do not build your Screen of the Mind, but continue in this way:

Day 1

As you continue to relax, picture a wave, of white light flowing through your body. Visualize it flowing through your toes; up the front of your body; up through your head; down your back and through the soles of your feet. Feel and visualize it moving back and forth in a great wave of soft, radiant light. As it bathes and fills your body, feel a change within yourself. Let the judgmental, negative thoughts flow out with the light. Feel the radiance and joy of the light filling your entire body.

Continue to breathe fully and deeply, circulating the light. If it is more difficult to experience the flow in any specific part of your body, pause and concentrate on that place until the light streams through freely.

When you are aware of the light radiance filling all parts of your body, allow it to flow out through your feet, your toes, your fingers, through the top of your head.

When your visualization is complete, open your eyes, experiencing a feeling of well-being and renewed vitality.

Repeat this entirely each day.

Days 2,3,4, 5 and 6

Each day write the experiences for that day. You may be tempted to summarize at the end of the week, but do not be tempted. You will find it valuable to write a full report of each day's visualizing.

Finding Order in Chaos

Central-Peripheral

You have been discovering your tranquil island and making it part of your days to find your center of quiet and stillness. Perhaps you are discovering also that visits to your island need not be confined to quiet, cloistered moments in time or place, but can be experienced in the midst of great tumult, or intense activity, bringing freedom from agitation, distraction, confusion. You can create order out of apparent chaos as you find a new way of viewing these turbulances, by understanding that they have a unique order all of their own.

Your role is to be still, and allow yourself to grasp this wider view and different order. With this comes a new perspective, a different centering position, a finer balance. You are aware not only of how you fit into the situation, but how all objects and persons around you fit into your space. It becomes an art of perceiving the total situation. The central-peripheral fields (you as center and the space around as periphery) become less separated. It is as if the fields merge into one space bubble around, with you at the center, a unified part of the total bubble. You begin to view discords as something to work through, rather than groping blindly in a chaotic world.

As you understand, and work through the storms of living in this way, you may be finding that states of inharmony still persist, but now you are in a different awareness and can move through the turbulances without reacting and taking on the conditions of the separate outer field. You do not have to struggle or resist. When you are struggling you are affected, but when your central and peripheral become more merged, you do not resist because there is nothing to resist. It is as if you, balanced in the center of a whirlwind, are observing and intensely aware of what is happening, but unshaken by the storm raging around you. When your center is separated from your peripheral field you are "living between two worlds" where the peripheral world becomes something external to be feared or avoided. However, living in the periphery and avoiding the center, is as lost between two worlds as the central-bound person, who has difficulty seeing the "big picture."

There is no center *and* periphery; there is only one field that is a blend of all awareness you hold of space before, behind, above, below and beside you. It is a totality of space which, when all of your senses are participating as one orchestra, becomes a great, blended harmonic whole instrument from which you bring forth your own unique music.

You are beginning to understand Spinoza when he said, "I saw that all the things I feared had nothing good or bad in them save as the mind was affected by them."

These are the ideas you will be working with during these days.

Day 1

This will be a day for becoming acquainted with your own central-peripheral process. You are to observe yourself throughout the day as you do many activities. What you will be observing is the flexibility of yourself in your space world. Observe and write your answers fully to the following questions:

1. As you are working with something where you are centrally concentrated, notice if you tend to block out all other things in order to concentrate, becoming completely oblivious to your environment.

2. If you are trying to concentrate where activities are occurring in your periphery, that cause you to be distracted and attend to them, are you inclined to become irritated or frustrated?

3. Or, are you able to maintain attention to the task with complete awareness of everything around you operating as part of you, but not distracting you. You find it a pleasant, or even neutral accompaniment to your thinking, as the distant sound of the surf rolls on, but is not necessary for your conscious attention?

4. Do you tend to be easily distracted by things around you so that as you are working on a centered project you find reason, constantly, for leaving it to do something else? Are the other things you choose, ones that involve movement of some kind? Are you able to concentrate in a near-space situation

only if the thing you are doing is intensely interesting to you? While you are doing it do you tend to "tune out" everything else around you?

5. Observe what things you find to do that really "turn you on." What things do you choose to do or prefer? Then analyze these things from the aspect of central-peripheral.

6. Do you get lost in your own thoughts, even in the midst of a conversation, and tune out people or things around you?

7. Observe how many things you tune out during the day. What are the things considered from the view of you in relation to your space bubble?

Day 2

Use the observations of yesterday to work with anything where you felt you were "stuck" or frustrated. As you work with those conditions, visualize yourself and the frustrating, distracting condition as part of a total operating space world. As you blend it into one whole, discover if your centering and balancing point emerges more clearly. Do the objects distracting you become less important viewed from the balanced center where you are dynamically occupied?

Write all of your observations in detail.

Day 3 Notice yourself at different times throughout this day, doing different activities.
Where is your position in your space bubble?
Are you located at the center, to the side,
toward the front, or the back? Does your
position change with the activity? How us-
able is the space around you? What is behind
you? Does your bubble continue the same
size throughout the day? Does it contract
and enclose you as you do various activities,
or does it expand and grow as large as infinity? Do you feel large or small in your
bubble? Does your size change from time to
time and from activity to activity?

Listen to different kinds of music, then
analyze what happens to your space, and to
you inside that space.

Write all of your observations and answer
all questions in detail.

This will be a day for observing yourself in different situations while driving your car. (If you will not be driving today you may exchange with another day.) While you are driving, try to become aware of yourself and your environment as one total unit. As you are experiencing the intense activity of a freeway, or city traffic, feel yourself a participant in the action, but also be very aware of your own balanced central position of calm control. Feel the pulse and rhythm around you, and yourself in unison with that pulse and rhythm. Visualize yourself as an integral part of the situation, rather than as an outsider pushed into an alien situation, having a separate rhythm at variance with the outer rhythm.

Day 4

As you practice these things, observe if you are able to react more easily to any problems arising around you. Notice if you recognize that the intensified pulse has a definite order and rhythm, one that is very different from your usual rhythm, but one that you can blend into and become part of. Notice as you adapt to this rhythm, making it your own rhythm, rather than struggling against it, if you handle the situation with less stress and fatigue than you ordinarily would have done.

Write all of your observations and experiences.

Day 5

This will be a day of practicing central-peripheral flexibility in a social situation, or, how to not get lost in one space! (Again, if you will not be socializing today, exchange with another day.) You will be working with the art of becoming aware of many things at once and doing many things at once. You will be practicing selecting what you want to become aware of around you while still remaining conscious of the total situation.

Choose different categories such as: colors, shapes, textures, sounds, movement, odors. Take each one, individually, around you to become aware of, and yet to not become distracted from the central activity involving you. For example, if you are conversing with someone, become aware of all the colors around you, while either conversing or listening. If you are attending a concert, notice how many categories you can be aware of and yet remain involved with the music. Practice turning on one sense, then turning it off and changing to another, then blending them all together.

Adapt these ideas to the social situation you are in, using the idea of expanding your attention.

Write all of your ideas, observations and experiences.

Day 6

Repeat any previous day that you feel could bring greater learning by repeating another time.

VIEW THREE

Changing the Centering

A N O T H E R
P O I N T   O F   V I E W

WEEK SEVEN
Changing the View of Yourself
and the World Around

WEEK EIGHT
Changing Your View of Others

WEEK NINE
Getting Unstuck
From One Point of View

Changing the View of Yourself and the World Around

Week Seven

As you use your Mind Screen to change undesirable conditions into desirable ones, you are using reversals, or opposites, for working with the principle of visualizing "another point of view."

This is a very important concept that can help you gain ease and freedom in all of your daily human relations. As you learn to shift your attention from one view to another one, you find flexibility within your own space. Gaining this wider view, helps you understand that things may appear one way at one time, but very different at another time. You learn not to get "stuck" in one point in space, so that seeing and understanding another point of view becomes part of your daily living.

During this week you will continue working with reversals. Each day observe and write down what you have visualized that day.

Days 1, 3, 5 and 6

Each day choose some everyday life happening, or any object around you, or an activity you may be doing, and imagine it is exactly the opposite of the way you usually see or do it. For example: imagine yourself in a situation that is the reverse of the one you are in, where you have feelings and wishes exactly contrary to your usual ones. Visualize, for example, what the situation would be if you had not gotten out of bed this morning. Or visualize what would happen in a certain situation if you had said, "no" instead of "yes", or vice versa. What if you were short instead of tall, or tall instead of short; blond instead of brunette, or the opposite. Use any of these suggestions to challenge your own visualization. Write the reversal as you visualize it, picturing in detail. Write what would be the result, or train of events that would occur as the result of such a reversed condition. As you visualize your reversals, let your mind and imagination roam freely and widely in the wonderful world of "Just Suppose."

Write about these two days at the end of each day. Visualize the sequence of the day in reverse. In other words, play the day backward. Start by visualizing the last thing you did before arriving where you are (bedtime). Visualize in detail, and work back through everything that happened, or that you experienced during the day, the things you said and did, until you arrive at waking up in the morning. When you finish reporting the day, note if there is anything you would have changed or done differently as you view it in this new way.

What have you learned form all of this? Do you feel, within your center, a more flexible, understanding, less prejudiced, less judicial *you?* Or do you find visualizing this way to be frustrating, threatening, or disturbing to your own comfortable, established point of view?

Write it!

Week Eight   Changing Your View of Others

If reversals are difficult for you to visualize, you
will have the same kinds of difficulties in all relationships with people. Most problems with others
are caused by the failure to visualize the feelings
and reactions of the other person. Even the ideal
state in the Golden Rule requires us to picture ourselves looking from the other person's view.

Your project this week is to use your imagination
to creatively study your "people" relationships and
how to encourage this gift of visualization in them
and in yourself.

Day 1 Build your Screen of the Mind's Eye and project on to it a picture of someone you know well. Visualize one thing about the person that you most admire. Picture the person doing this admirable thing, or activity. See it vividly and enjoy it. Next, imagine how you can use some part of this admired quality to enhance and increase your own effectiveness. Visualize yourself having this quality, or doing this activity. Write all of this down — step-by-step, following your pictures.

Day 2 Use the same person of Day 1. Again, build your Mind Screen, but this time project the person doing or being something you find least admirable that limits the person's effectiveness. Visualize in detail. Now, erase the picture and project the person reversing that quality to one that would redirect him/her to greater accomplishment or enjoyment of living. Hold that picture in your mind, and think of ways (without being critical, judgmental, or officious) of helping him/her to make this picture a reality. Write in detail as you visualized.

Build your Mind Screen. Project on to it the person you find the least compatible with you. Visualize this person clearly in full detail including the things you dislike. Now erase your screen. Project the person again, but this time release from judicial judging and select one thing about him/her that you find admirable. Picture this quality. Now visualize how, in the future, you can use this picture to change your view of this person by magnifying the desirable quality and minimizing the offensive ones.

Day 3

Combine Days 1 and 2, using a person of the opposite sex from the one you chose originally. Write what you visualize.

Day 4

Combine Days 1 and 2, using a person from a different age group than your original person. Please write!

Day 5

During this day review back through your week and write down at least one instance where your ability to visualize from the point of view of the other person either improved, or rescued a situation.

Day 6

Week *Nine* Getting Unstuck
From One Point of View

In your previous two projects of Changing the Centering, you may have experienced frustrations while trying to shake off your own fixed habits, and climb out of your "comfortable rut" to see from another wider direction or view.

In "comfortable rut" thinking we become buried in the same attitudes and habits of thinking. We tend to continue using the same verbal grouping patterns for thinking and solving problems. As we use visualization, we are able to see the patterns rearranged and regrouped. With these projects you have been exploring many ways of encouraging visual thinking through grouping and reorganizing. This week will be devoted to observing how blindly we accept obvious approaches when solving problems; then finding different ways of visualizing, rather than using the most probable solution.

Below you will find a puzzle. Without lifting your pencil from the paper draw four straight connected lines which will cross through all nine dots, but through each dot only once.

If this puzzle is familiar to you, using the four lines, then, by applying the same instructions, cross through all nine dots using only three lines.

As you work with this, study your process. Are you falling into the "rut trap" by doing rut thinking and restricting your visualizing so that you cannot "see" another point of view?

Here is another challenge for your visualization using a changed view:

Take five matches (or toothpicks). Break one match in half and use only one half of it. You will be using four and one half matches to make a figure that looks like the following one pictured:

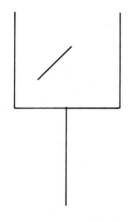

This figure represents a cocktail glass with a stem on the glass. The half match represents the olive inside the glass. Your problem is: by moving only two matches, finish with an identical cocktail glass (the same shape, size and stem), but the olive will be outside the glass instead of inside as when you started. You cannot break any other matches than the olive match. You must use all 4½ matches.

If you have difficulty with the solution, you probably are lost in the rut. Quiet your mind and allow your visualization to give you a new view.

Day 3

Using rut thinking we approach problem situations with the same stereotyped solutions. Even though these solutions do not always produce the best results, we continue repeating them over and over, rather than regrouping and visualizing from another view. In the following situations find five different solutions for the problem. Do not restrict your visualization by using obvious solutions. Turn off your judging and "no-no-ing" too soon, and think of unusual or humorous ways of solving it. Step out of your "comfortable rut" so you are not stuck in one view.

The situation is: You live in an apartment complex where the son of your landlord plays his stereo recordings (usually "hard rock") until two or three o'clock in the morning, while you are trying to sleep. What solutions would you have for getting him to stop? Visualize and write five different solutions.

Day 4

Here is another situation: You are making a long cross-country trip by plane. The plane is filled to capacity, with no seats available for you to change to another seat. Seated next to you is a person of the opposite sex, much older than you. In spite of all your efforts to discourage the person, he/she talks to you constantly, ignoring your attempts to read or sleep. The person is slightly deaf, so speaks very loudly. You have many hours

ahead with this situation. What would you
do to discourage him/her?

Visualize and write (in detail) your five
different solutions.

Choose a problem that you presently have
that concerns you, one in which a number of
different people are involved. Visualize the
problem from the view of each one of the
other persons — step over into their shoes.
Write your visualization of the problem seen,
first, from your own view, then from that
of each other person.

Day 5

Carefully study and review your work for the
five days. Ask yourself if your solutions are
obvious and stereotyped, or have you allowed
yourself to peek over the top of your rut to
find a new view.

Day 6

Re-View

WEEK TEN
Re-View

Week Ten   **Re-View**

This week will be devoted to reviewing all of the preceding weeks. Review one or two View weeks each day to find if you are, or are not, making the thinking of each week part of your daily life. As you review each one, if you find that you have not really made some part of it a very real part of your thinking, then work with that part during the day. Be aware of how it fits in to your total visualization.

Review View I (Orchestration of the Senses); Week 1 — The Orchestra.

Think about it, analyze yourself and write if the ideas are an important part of your activities. Have they subconsciously affected your view of things around you, or have you slid back into your comfortable rut by either ignoring, or forgetting to use them?

Review View I — Week 2 — The Concert Master (Visual Principles for Living).

What about it? Have these three principles become part of *you* or do you tend to fall back into the old ways of: Judging, "no-noing", or verbalizing where you very easily could be visualizing? Write what you think about it.

Review View I — Week 3 — Combining Orchestra and Concert Master (Living This Moment). *Day 2*

Are you *really* using it? Are you finding a different kind of tranquility through feeling and visualizing, "Today is today, this moment is this moment and I will accomplish what is here-and-now," or are you still in the trap of jumping and lunging? Are you trying to catch up with what you should have done in the past here-and-nows (where you really never were), or are you projecting into the future impossibly packed, jammed here-and-nows (where you really never will be)? Study it carefully, then ask yourself if the thinking has become part of your awareness. Study and visualize on this day, then write what you think about it.

**Day 3**

Review View II (Inner Visual Centering): Week 4 — Island of Tranquility and Screen of the Mind. Also review Week 5 — Visualizing Light.

Review them both. Find if you are using them throughout your days to ease the turbulances around you. Or are you saying, "I just don't have time to do that!" Study and become aware of how these visual guides bring new extensions to time and new dimensions to space. Really work with them this day. Write what you are discovering.

**Day 4**

Review View II — Week 6 — Finding Order in Chaos (Central-Peripheral).

Are you able to find order in the midst of, what appear to be, chaotic conditions around you? Are you refusing to allow the peripheral conditions to impose their disturbing arrhythmia upon you? Or, instead, are you finding a new center, a new order and rhythm, that bring you and the peripheral condition into a total, more harmonic space? Are you beginning to glimpse the larger picture, the total space bubble, and your center in that space? Are you more able to expand your attention as you attend to many things simultaneously? Are you able to flexibly move from one sensory awareness to another, then blend them into one unified whole?

Thoughtfully work with these significant ideas, then write about your adventures.

Review View III (Changing the Centering —
Another Point of View); Week 7 — Changing
Your View of Yourself and the World Around.
Also review Week 8 — Changing Your View
of Others.

Day 5

Review them both. Are you finding more
tolerance, more compassion within yourself
as you discover another view, another aspect
in situations, people, and yourself than you
formerly found in your structured peep-hole
view? Or are you still dropping into negative-
ly programming people, situations, and yourself as you visualize but one view?

Write what you are thinking.

Review View III — Week 9 — Getting Unstuck
from One Point of View.

Day 6

Review what your thinking was with this.
Are you discovering that you behave like the
fly, buzzing blindly at the known dimension
of the windowpane, with the greater dimension of the open window at the side? Does
this reveal the idea that there might be many
new dimensions every day that you are miss-
ing by restricting your visualizing?

Write what you think about this.

Visualizing Other Spaces and Times

WEEK ELEVEN

Memory Pictures
Three Months to One Year

WEEK TWELVE

Memory Pictures
*Exploring the Space Bubble —
Far, Mid, Near Space*

WEEK THIRTEEN

Memory Pictures
Now Holds Past and Future

Week Eleven

Memory Pictures

Three Months to One Year

During these weeks, much of your time has been devoted to finding how to live and become more aware in each *now* moment. You have worked with the view that the present moment holds the shape and form of all future moments. If you visualize your present desires, hopes and dreams delayed to some future perfection, or if you are controlled or restricted by some past imperfection or perfection, you are not living and experiencing fully in any time or space. The more you can live in your present time with all sensory modes attuned to the larger picture, the more your orchestra records for use in future days.

In the three weeks of this View you will be exploring past memory pictures to recapture lost parts of yourself; to find what those parts have contributed to your present moments; to find what you have recorded through your senses, and to discover where there are blank spaces in your recording. As you explore your thought and memory pictures in this way, you can find which ones appeared acceptable to you in that time and space, but in this *now* space and time, no longer make sense. You can decide which ones should be erased from your Screen of Mind and replaced with ones more useful and valuable.

You will use this thinking, during this week, to explore memory pictures. Choose ones that occurred from three months to one year ago. Each day observe and write down what you have visualized on that day.

Sit quietly, close your eyes and rest. In your mind's eye picture a visit made to a friend's house. As you revisit, visualize vividly, involving all of your senses. Does attention to any particular sensory mode evoke more images than attention to others? Which ones are most difficult to recapture? Which ones appear vividly, and which ones appear vaguely? Are you moving around in your picture the same way that you moved in the original visit? Do you have difficulty visualizing your own movements, or those of your friend? Do you see color in your picture? Can you hear conversation? Can you recapture the emotions and feelings of that time? As you picture this event in the *now*, are there any parts of the picture that appear fuzzy or incomplete because of your limited awareness in some sensory mode? Is there anything you would do differently Now?

Write all of your memory pictures in detail.

Day 1

Sit quietly, close your eyes and rest. In your mind's eye picture a trip taken either alone, with another person, or with a group of people. Once again, record all of your senses, all of the motion and movement of yourself and others that you can visualize. Notice the changes in scenery, the shadows of light and dark and color as the time of day changes. Ask and give answers to the same questions as you did on Day 1. Write vividly as you visualize.

Day 2

Day 3   Sit quietly, close your eyes and rest. In your mind's eye picture a party you attended. Do you see color, action, movement; hear music, conversation, laughter? Does all of it appear real? Record all of your senses. As you picture this event in the *now*, do any parts of the picture appear fuzzy or incomplete because of your limited awareness in some particular sensory mode? Is there anything you would do differently in the *now?* Write your visualizing.

Day 4   Sit quietly, close your eyes and rest. In your mind's eye picture a lecture, a concert, a ballet, a workshop, or an opera that you attended. Bring in all of your senses and visualize the movement. Make the same observations, and ask the same questions as you did on Day 3. Write your observations.

Sit quietly, close your eyes and rest. Visual- *Day 5*
ize a day spent where you felt least in harmony with yourself and others around you.
As you visualize and recapture a total sensory awareness, can you find why you felt
that way? Was it because of limitations in
your own awareness? Could you have changed
it in some way by becoming more aware of
any particular sensory mode?

Repeat Day 5, except to visualize a day spent *Day 6*
where you felt *most* in harmony with yourself and others around you.

Write — Write all of it — each day!

Week Twelve

Memory Pictures

Exploring the Space Bubble —
Far, Mid, Near Space

You are continuing the exploration of memory pictures to find what they have contributed to your present moments, and then to carry that learning into future moments.

In your last week you found how much, or how little you had recorded through your senses, also the things you had appreciated and the ones ignored.

This week you will be exploring the mutiple dimensions of far, mid, and near spaces, and how they influence your orientation in your visual space bubble.

The boundaries of these spaces overlap, but, generally, we can say that:

Near space — is all that space just inside the slightly outstretched arms.

Mid space — is all that space from slightly outstretched arms to five to eight feet.

Far space — is all that space from five to eight feet, on out to the moon and all other celestial bodies.

Since human eyes are located in the front of the head we tend to think of our visual space world located out in front of us, but, as the word "bubble" implies, it not only encompasses front, but also side, top, bottom and back dimensions.

Each one of us has visual space preferences. This would be the space where, given our choice, we feel most visually comfortable, happy and at ease.
In this chosen space we tend to observe and record more information than we do within the others. If we are far-space oriented we may have difficulty concentrating in near space, and so our observations at near will reveal our visual limitations. If we are near-space people, we may feel happy with our bubble snuggled closely around us, and thus observe less of what goes on "out there". Our visualizations will reflect our limited view of the larger picture.

Mid space is the visual avenue that must be traveled as attention is moved from near to far, or from far to near. If there is difficulty making an easy transition, the journey may be simplified by making a non-stop hop from one space platform to the other. The blanks in recording will show what has been ignored or "turned off".

Our own personal visual space bubble fluctuates. It expands and contracts from day to day, even from moment to moment, depending upon our activities and interests, or our feelings and tensions of the moment. At times we experience an expansive space; at other times, a tight, small space. Of paramount importance with this learning is gaining flexibility in the multiple dimensions of space; of seeing the larger, whole picture. The more flexibly we can move throughout our total space bubble, the more information we record each moment, and avoid "getting stuck" in one space.

You will use this thinking during this week to explore more memory pictures. This time you will visualize pictures that occurred not more recently than one year ago, on back to childhood. Observe and record not only with all of your sensory modes aware, but tune in to all parts of the far, mid, and near spaces you are experiencing. Particularly note and observe the spaces that you are inclined to avoid or ignore. In what parts of the space do you tend to linger? Do you get "stuck" in any parts? In what space does your visualization have "holes"?

Each day observe and write down what you have visualized for that day.

Day 1   Find a position of rest. Close your eyes. Visualize a special room of your childhood. As you look at the room, what are you doing? Are you moving around? Are you playing, sleeping? Locate the windows and doors. As you look out of them, what do you see? Bring in all of your senses to find what images they bring to you. Can you recall walls, furniture, floor, pictures on the wall? Note and observe, making comments on the spaces as suggested in the introduction. What emotions do you experience as you revisit this room?

Day 2   Rest, close your eyes. Visualize a special event of your teens. Bring in all sensory and all spaces as you did on Day 1.

Day 3   Rest, close your eyes. Visualize an emotional experience of great consequence. Include all spaces and sensory modes.

Rest, close your eyes. Visualize an experience that brought great embarrassment to you. Include space and sensory as before.

Day 4

Rest, close your eyes. Visualize a highly humorous situation in which you were involved that you still find amusing as you recall and visualize it. Don't forget space and sensory.

Day 5

Rest, close your eyes. Visualize a memory picture of your own choice that will clearly include all senses and all spaces. Preferably choose one from your late childhood.

Day 6

Write! Write!

Week Thirteen

Memory Pictures
Now Holds Past and Future

You have been studying past memories to find
what your senses have recorded within your space
bubble dimensions. If your awareness was limited
in any sensory or in any space, then your *now* visualizations will reflect those limitations.

If you are "stuck" in any sensory mode or in
any space, it will be difficult to release from reliance
on those modes or spaces so that visual picturing
can emerge unencumbered, free from dependence.
This is a necessary step toward the greater refinement of View V where even visual picturing itself
is sublimated, and the silent non-picturing aspect of
visualization is revealed.

This time your exploration of memory pictures
will encompass the long line of time, how the past

has brought you to *now* and *now* carries you into the future. Actually they are not three different times, but are one time in a continuum, and that time is called *"now"*. All that has happened in the past, or will happen in the future, are but pictures that exist in your own mind, and they exist in the *now*. You can think of *past-future-present* as parts of one greatly expanded *now,* in which you can produce, use, change, or erase any picture of the past or future.

With this project you will be using all of the visual thinking and projects you have been pursuing to find what you are learning and applying. You are directed to work with this project in a different way: Day 1 will be divided into two parts: Part 1 to be completed one day, then Part 2 to be completed on the following day. You are to work with Days 3 and 4 following the same plan.

It is important that you clearly visualize the following instruction:

Please do not read through Day 2, or Day 4 before working with Days 1 and 3. Read each project on the day of work, and not before. Pre-reading the second part will influence your thinking on the day you are working.

(**Part 1**) — Feel quiet and relaxed. Visualize a memory picture of any event, at any time in your life (up to a month ago), that you feel has particularly influenced your life in the *now*. Choose a memory picture that, at that time, appeared to be fortunate, happy, very "good". Visualize it vividly from a personal view, reliving it, as nearly as possible, in that time and space. How do you feel it has influenced your *now*? What influence do you feel it holds over your future? As you picture all of this, please write the senses you are most and least aware of, and the spaces (far, mid, near) you are most and least aware of. Complete writing all of this before reading or continuing Part 2 of this project.

Day 1

(**Part 2 of Day 1**) — Feel quiet and relaxed. Now, rest and feel your own visual centering as you allow yourself to "get out of your own way" to view the same memory picture of Day 1, observing it impersonally from a new view of neither "good", nor "bad". Use all of your visual principles of:

Day 2

1. Watch — don't analyze — simply observe.
2. Let go of judicial judgment — view through unprejudiced eyes.

As you visualize from an impersonal, changed view, bringing your picture into the present, then projecting the changes this "happening" can make on your future, is your view of its influence, on your present and future, different from your first visualization?

Does the memory picture still appear as "good" to you; does it have aspects of "bad"; or can you "get out of your own way" to impersonalize it, so it appears neither entirely bad or entirely good? Can you view it with an understanding of the place and function it occupies and performs in your *now* and the Future? Write all of this down. When you finish writing, review these instructions to see if you have considered all of the suggested aspects.

Day 3

(Part 1) —Feel quiet and relaxed. Visualize a memory picture of any event, at any time in your life (to within a month ago) that you feel has particularly influenced your life in the *now*. Choose a memory picture that, at that time, appeared to be unfortunate, unhappy, not "good". Visualize it vividly from a personal view, reliving it, as nearly as possible, in that time and space. How do you feel it has influenced your *now?* What influence do you feel it holds over your future? As you picture all of this, please write the senses you are most and least aware of, and the spaces (far, mid, near) you are most and least aware of. Complete writing all of this down before reading or continuing Part 2 of this project.

OTHER SPACES AND TIMES

(Part 2 of Day 3) — Feel quiet and relaxed. Now, rest and feel your own visual centering as you allow yourself to "get out of your own way" to view the same memory picture of Day 3, observing it impersonally from a new view of neither "good", nor "bad". Use all of your visual principles of:

1. Watch — don't analyze — simply observe.
2. Let go of judicial judgment — view through unprejudiced eyes.

As you visualize from an impersonal, changed view, bringing your picture into the present, then projecting the changes this "happening" can make on your future, is your view of its influence, on your present and future, different from your first visualization? Does the memory picture still appear as "bad" to you; does it have aspects of "good"; or can you "get out of your own way" to impersonalize it, so it appears neither entirely bad, nor entirely good? Can you view it with an understanding of the place and function it occupies and performs in your *now* and the Future? Write all of this down. When you finish writing, review these instructions to see if you have considered all of the suggested aspects.

Day 5

Early on this day carefully review in your mind how you have been working with this project, and what you have been learning. Then dismiss it completely from your logical, verbal, conscious mind. During this day enjoy observing without actively making yourself think about observing. Allow yourself to discover new spaces, new sensory experiences, new quietnesses within your own center. Trust yourself — don't argue with yourself — open yourself to new spaces, new senses.

Write how this affects you.

Day 6

During the first four days of this week you observed your memory pictures by contrasting and comparing them from first, a personal view of either bad or good, to second, a less personal, less judicial, less verbal view. The thought was to find how those pictures fit into your living as a long line, or continuum of *now* holding both the past and future. You observed your pictures to find an awareness of greater space and sensory expansion through noting the spaces and senses you tended either to stick in or to avoid.

On Day 5 you dismissed the project from your logical, verbal conscious mind and turned it over to your visual, intuitive, subconscious mind as you allowed the visual learning to continue and refine. Today please make the following observations, and answer the questions, writing all of your impressions:

1. Carefully read the introduction for Week 13.
2. Carefully read everything that you have written.
3. Contemplate on what you have written to find if you have deleted any of your visual thinking.
4. Make certain your written observations are not obscure, nondefinitive generalizations.
5. Consider if anything of value came out of the contemplative, subconscious thinking of Day 5.

Answer the following questions:

1. Did the work you did this week bring a fuller understanding of the long line of *now-ness*?
2. Were you able to make a more definitive contrast between the personal and impersonal views from Day 1 to Day 2 and Day 3 to Day 4?
3. Has your awareness of your space bubble expanded working with this View IV?
4. Has your total sensory awareness increased working with this View IV?

The Director of the Orchestra

VISION AND VISUALIZATION

WEEK FOURTEEN
Matching the Outer and Inner Ears

WEEK FIFTEEN
Turning the Inner Verbalizer
On and Off

WEEK SIXTEEN
The Inner Silence of Visualization

Week Fourteen — Matching the Outer and Inner Ears

As you have reflected on, and have written all of the previous Views, making visual picturing part of your daily living, and have practiced the principles of: withholding judgment; trusting and not arguing with your visualizing; seeing but not saying; bringing yourself back into the here and now; developing an island of tranquility to rest in, even in life's daily problems; circulating light throughout your body; finding order in the midst of apparent chaos; changing your view of yourself and others to see problems reversed; feeling a nowness of time that included past and future as a continuum; expanding your space bubble for a wider, fuller awareness of the space around you — all of these many Views should be bringing a new view of the world, people, and even changing the view of yourself.

As a companion on this journey of discovery, you have had the orchestral music of your senses, ever expanding into a richer, fuller symphony, preparing for the appearance of the Director to move the many pieces of the orchestra into one blended magnificent instrument, to produce the celestial music of visualization.

Perhaps you are discovering that many of the seemingly essential needs of the past are dropping away and disappearing, of their own accord, because they are no longer needed. They actually, now, may be getting in the way of your new visual thinking and awareness. Others, however, more tenacious, may continue to dig in and hang on. One of the most persistent of these "hanger-onners" is inner speech, the little inner verbalizer that prompts and accompanies much of visual imagery, as it argues, cajoles, and wheedles. The roots of visualization rest deeply in visual picturing, but as the process develops and refines, it is necessary for the picturing stage to release from verbal prompting, until a state is reached, where even the images fade and recede leaving a dynamic silence — a nonintellectual awareness. Verbalizing can be a valuable companion to visualizing when it can be flexibly turned on or off as desired, but when it becomes the tyrannical Director, all parts of the symphony are limited, stuck at the slower rate of the verbal tyrant.

Also, because you are so busy talking to yourself, you have limited time and opportunity to actually listen to other people, and probably are not really listening to yourself. When speaking and listening become a unity, your understanding grows, of how and what you are thinking.

Your work this week will be concentration in controlling your verbal tyrant, first by listening to yourself, and then listening to your thoughts.

This will be a day to find if you really hear and recognize your own voice. Read something aloud, or preferably, recite a memorized poem, or a favorite piece of prose. As you recite, or read, listen closely to the resonance, vibration, range, quality, and flexibility of your voice. Make the following observations:

Day 1

1. Are you more interested in the words you are speaking than in what your voice is doing?
2. Is your production of words clear or fuzzy?
3. Does your voice express what you are feeling, or is it flat and monotonous?
4. As you speak aloud, do you hear your inner voice speaking also?
5. Is your inner voice saying the same thing as your outer voice?
6. When you stop reading or reciting, does the inner voice stop also, or does it continue on with other words of its own?

Practice all of this with other poems or prose until you feel you are truly hearing both your outer and inner voices and becoming acquainted with them.

When you are satisfied that the two voices are in unison, begin alternating by reading a few lines aloud, then letting the inner voice recite the next few lines. Listen carefully for the many aspects of each voice. Does the unison begin to sound like *you*?

Practice throughout the day, stopping at intervals to write all of your discoveries.

Day 2

Because many of the essential characteristics of sound, such as: duration, frequency, and intensity, combined with the qualities of resonance, pitch and range, are all shared equally by language and music, and both of these are dependent on the effective use of rhythm, much can be learned about these essential qualities by studying the musical voice. Many persons are unable to use their singing voice. Perhaps early in life they have become self-conscious when their musical vocalizing met such put-down remarks as: "I didn't know we had frogs around here", or "What you need is a little bird seed."

Matching the internal and external voices, rhythms and frequencies are vital for visual shifting. When these processes are not matching, these mismatches are responsible for many visual-verbal "hang-ups". For example, the problems of stammerers and stutterers, the arhythmia of Parkinsonism, the propulsive movements of the hyper-active child, the insensitivity of the dyslexic to the rhythm and flow of language, the poor discrimination of the disabled speller to emphasis and accent in the syllable — any of these symbolic mismatches reveal the incongruence between internal and external rhythms.

So, during this day, even if you feel there is no singing voice worse than your own, forget all of your previous "put-downs", sing and listen to yourself:

1.   Start by singing a song, any song that you know either from days of the past or from present time. If you don't know all of the lyrics, fill in with any words or syllables such as, "la, la, lo, lu, lu" — but sing aloud. Open

your mouth and throat and sing! As you sing, listen whether your inner voice is singing along with you.

2.   When you have finished the song, repeat it, but this time sing two lines, then let your inner voice sing two lines. Listen to how it sounds. Is it, perhaps, not as repulsive as you had expected?   Finish the song in this way.

3.   Choose either a new song (if you know one), or repeat the first one. This time let the inner voice start the song for two lines, then you pick up the next two passages. Continue to the end of the song. Make the following observations:

>Did you stay in tune?
>Were you able to hear and follow the rising and falling of the song?
>Did your two voices match in rhythmical flow, or did you feel a mismatch between the two, such as a tendency for one or the other to speed ahead or to slow down?

Continue practicing singing throughout the day, both in and outside. Practice in different spaces, such as small or large rooms. Carefully observe the unity, or lack of unity between the two voices. Write down all of your musical discoveries.

Day 3

On this day start by reading or reciting as you did on Day 1, but proceed in this way:

Place a hand over one ear as you read or recite aloud. Read two or three lines, listening carefully to the sound production as you have done previously. Then cover the other ear and listen to the sound. Does the sound match from ear to ear in highness, lowness, resonance, loudness, softness, pitch? If they do not match, how do they differ? Compare alternately to find mismatches. (At this point it would be wise to make notes of your discoveries so you won't forget about them when you write later). When you have made observations for a few minutes, cover both ears and find what differences you find from:

1. When both ears were open.
2. When either one ear or the other was closed.
3. What is happening to your inner voice during all of this discovering?

At another time during the day, repeat the above procedure by singing instead of reading, or reciting:

1. With one ear covered.
2. With the other ear covered.
3. With both ears covered.

Make your observations as suggested when you were reciting.

This will be a day of practicing voice matching in a social situation. (If it is not convenient to socialize on this day, you may exchange with one of the other days during this week, when you may find yourself with other people.)

Observe your own voice as you are speaking in company. Does your voice sound the same to you as it did when you were reading or reciting aloud to yourself? What differences do you notice in quality, tone, etc.? Is your voice different when you are conversing with different people? For example, with different sexes, or ages? Do you find yourself continuously talking in order to avoid an embarrassing silence? Do you listen and follow another person's conversation to a conclusion, or do you continuously break in with your own verbal promptings or comments? Even though you may be outwardly silent, do you have most of your listening preoccupied with your own inner verbalizer?

If you find your tendency is to over-verbalize in company, where you find yourself opening most conversations if there is a lull, then practice letting another person start the conversation. If, conversely, your tendency is to let others open the conversation, then practice opening it yourself. How does your voice sound to you in either one of these situations? Do you sound like *you* to yourself?

When you are by yourself, write down all of the observations and discoveries you have made.

Day 5

This will be a day of matching your visual pictures with your verbal tonal qualities. You will be using color for this. Start by making a visual picture in which one color predominates. Describe it aloud. For example, you might say, "I see a *green* garden." Let your voice describe the color *green* as you see it in your picture. It might be a wonderful, lush greenness, vibrant and filled with all the fresh green of spring. Let your voice speak the word "Green", giving it this meaning.

Next, let your voice intone, "Green" as a hideous, slimy green. Continue to use the same color for each change of verbal intonation, but watch each time as your voice changes the color, if your picture changes with it. Does it change to match the verbal description?

Practice this with other colors and other situations, scenes, or things. Each time use different intonations for the color, and watch the pictures change to match.

After you have practiced this a few times, alternate saying the color aloud, then have the inner voice speak the color. Note if the inner and outer voices match in rhythm and intonation. Does the inner voice tend to editorialize on its own?

Write down your observations or matching or mis-matching.

This will be a day of noting changes in accent or emphasis, and in variations and modulations of tone.

Practice saying sentences, changing emphasis on different words. For example:

<u>Scott</u> did not buy that car. (Someone else did)

Scott <u>did</u> not buy that car. (He didn't?)

Scott did <u>not</u> buy that car. (I disagree)

Scott did not <u>buy</u> that car. (He only leased it)

Scott did not buy <u>that</u> car. (He bought another one)

Scott did not buy that <u>car.</u> (He bought a boat instead)

As you vary the emphasis, note the changed picture it brings each time. Alternate listening to your outer voice, followed by your inner. Do they match? Write down what you have learned.

Week Fifteen

Turning the Inner Verbalizer On and Off

Now that you have become better acquainted with your outer and inner voices, have listened attentively, and have practiced matching them to become a team, this unity allows you more flexible control in turning the inner verbalizer on when you wish to listen to it, or in silencing it when you wish to attend to visual imagery. You are learning that the inner voice doesn't have to be a tyrant, but that it can become a valuable inner counselor as you use the art of listening to it. This week will be devoted to these two arts of listening to the inner counselor, then silencing it to join with you in enjoying the visual pictures. Gaining mastery of picturing without words is an essential step to the dynamic inner silence of visualization.

Day 1

Find a place where you can relax and be quiet. Close your eyes. Have your inner verbalizer start saying the alphabet very slowly. As it speaks each letter, you are to visualize and erect each one vertically, side by side in a long horizontal row. When they are all aligned, tell the inner voice that it is to choose one letter in random order, but not to verbalize it to you. Instruct your inner assistant that it is not to give you clues about the letters by speaking them, that this is the game of "See-Don't-Say", that you must visualize without verbal clues. Then rest your eyes and mind and allow the letters on each side of the given letter to appear. If the verbalizer insists on assisting you verbally, continue to instruct it to be quiet, as you proceed with your visualizing.

The next step is to erase the previous alphabet, then rebuild the row. Tell your inner assistant that this time you will be visualizing the alphabet letters one by one without any verbal assistance from it. As you visualize each letter you will hand the letter to your assistant, who will silently place each letter either in a horizontal row, or in a vertical column, whichever it finds most pleasing. If it surreptitiously sneaks a word in here and there, continue reprimanding it, telling it not to cheat, but to play the game of "See-Don't-Say". Write down all of your experiences.

DIRECTOR OF THE ORCHESTRA

Find a place of rest and close your eyes. In your mind prepare to meet someone. This may be either a social or a business situation. Tell your verbalizer that you will be rehearsing, in your mind, where it will be located, what it will be about, what you will be saying to the person, etc. Tell the verbalizer that it will be the leader, that as it verbally describes the situation, you will be following the verbal description with pictures. Let the verbalizer babble on, as much as it wishes, as you attentively follow with picturing. When it is satisfied that the event is completed, tell it now to be silent throughout as you turn on the pictures of the event from beginning to end. All it has to do is watch the pictures you are making from its verbal description. If it attempts to cut in and verbally correct you on any picture, admonish it to be quiet, that you are leading with pictures. Explain that it will have time at the end for corrections. When you have completed your visual description, listen attentively to what it has to say about anything you deleted or changed. Really listen! Write down all of your adventures.

Day 2

**Day 3**

During this day listen to three different kinds of music: first from an early classical composer such as: Handel, Beethovan, Mozart, Bach; then from an early modern composer such as: Debussy, Stravinsky, Ravel; and finally from a jazz composer in any jazz era. Don't choose music from TV, but choose ones from radio, tape or phonograph, without lyrics. You and your inner assistant and counselor are going to visualize the images the music brings. These may be scenes, form, or color. You may experience any one, or all of these. Your inner assistant should first describe what it sees as you visualize, then be silent and follow as you visualize, then the two of you picture in unison. The images may occur as color flowing around you, or form evolving and disappearing. Allow whatever appears, to move and expand. Feel the wordless, synchronized rhythm. Suddenly, at regular intervals during the music, ask your assistant to describe in words what it is experiencing, then just as suddenly, instruct it to be silent. Write down your discoveries.

Day 4

Repeat Day 1, carefully noting and writing down if there is anything different occurring in each phase of the project.

Find a quiet place, close your eyes and rest. Today you will work on a problem that has eluded your attempts to find a satisfactory solution. You may choose the problem from any department in your life that you wish to explore. Follow the same format as you used on Day 2, of preparing to meet someone. Instruct your assistant that you will be playing the "follow the leader" game again, that it will be the first leader as you follow, and that it will be verbally describing the problem as you follow with pictures. When it has finished, reverse your roles as you re-picture from the verbal description while it follows your pictures. Then ask your inner counselor to make some suggestions about solutions. Allow it to discuss any ideas it may have, no matter how ridiculous, or impractical they may sound to you. You are simply to listen, and picture the solution in whatever form it comes to you, following the sequence as you did with the music game of Day 3. When your counselor has run out of ideas, both of you be silent and allow pictures to evolve, or just be silent as you allow the ideas to "soak". When you feel the rhythmical unity of the silence between you, dismiss the problem from your mind. Write all of your experiences, and all of your ideas.

Day 5

Repeat Day 5 to find what has happened during the "soaking" time. Did new solutions occur? Did any of the impractical or ridiculous ideas of Day 5 reveal a different aspect? Were you able to feel the silence as a rhythmical unity? Write all of your observations.

Week Sixteen

The Inner Silence of Visualization

During these days of slowing the incessant, arguing activity of your verbalizer, then guiding it to become your inner companion and counselor, you have moved away from conscious awareness of each individual sense, into the experience of an expanded, greater whole. This may appear as one unified sense, where visual images move in linked sequence, then disappear into the silence. It is as if you and your inner companion are spectators, moving on tip-toe, silently observing the unified rhythmical process.

Within this deep silence of the quiet mind, you perhaps hear, as from afar, the sublime music of visualization, as the master conducts the orchestra, uniting it into one perfectly balanced instrument.

You may find not only a silence of your verbalizer, but a silence of your body, of your thoughts, of all striving. In this silence, thinking does not stagnate and cease, but a different thinking emerges from that usually considered thought. It is a heightened and vivid awareness, a feeling of arriving at the center of your own true wisdom, a release from the imprisoning cage of time and space.

At this stage of your visual evolution, you are finding it unnecessary to work and strive at things because they seem to happen without effort. You are learning the true meaning of "allowing" as your conscious striving to achieve things shifts to effortlessly allowing things to be achieved in you. These are the things you will be perceiving and knowing as you work with this last project.

Build your mind screen and your island, or use whatever you have found brings you a tranquil and still mind. Close your eyes and enjoy the tranquility. Feel you and your inner companion breathing in unison. Let no thoughts come into your mind, just feel the rhythmical rising and falling of your breath. Notice the resting pause between the two breaths. Rest upon it each time, as if you are resting on a billowy, downy substance of white luminosity. Visualize the radiance of the substance as you feel it envelop and enfold you in its incredible softness. Appreciate the pause between breaths to vitalize and refreshen you. As you continue to visualize and feel the substance, slowly release yourself and allow it to disappear into infinite space. Release yourself from awareness of your breathing, then from all of your senses, and finally from all visual imagery. Rest in the silence of infinity, remaining as long as the silence endures.

Practice this two or three times during this day, writing down your observations. As you repeat the project, note any changes that occur in allowing the release into the silence.

Day 1

Choose a quiet place, close your eyes and find the silence. Visualize a square, a circle and a triangle. Remind your inner companion (if, perhaps, it might be tempted), there must be no labeling, only picturing. Let the forms interact. If nothing happens, just wait and watch. As the shapes emerge, let your gaze play around them, moving as they move. Be aware of the background, allowing it to change with the shapes. View them from many angles, noticing if they are flat or have dimension. Do they move and tumble, interweaving with one another? Do they change in size or position in space relative to you, in far, mid or near space? Watch as long as you wish, then turn a bright beam of light on the figures. Let the light follow the shapes as they move and tumble. Finally let the beam extend miles and eons into space as the figures ride the light and disappear into the distance. Let the light follow the shapes and disappear. Now rest in the remaining velvety darkness and silence.

Repeat this once during the day, writing all of your observations.

Find your silence, close your eyes and rest. You and your inner companion choose a beach to walk on. Choose one with spectacular waves that roll and crash on the beach. You are walking barefoot just at the edge of the crashing waves, feeling the cold sand under your feet, and between your toes. Feel the contrast between the warmth of the sun and the cool of the air. Be vividly aware of the air and sun moving around and through you. Hear a glorious symphony of music soaring to a mighty crescendo as one great wave crashes on the beach, enveloping you and carrying you with it. At first you are aware of the change from golden sun warmth to icy cold water. You fight for breath as the sound is deafening in your ears. Then, unexpectedly, you find yourself riding on top of the wave, as it carries you ever farther to sea. The music diminishes to a lullaby, filling all space about the undulating cradle in which you rest, until you are softly deposited back on the beach. You lie there with the cool sand, water and air around and under you, the warm golden sun and music filling your body, feeling yourself part of all nature. Then slowly all images drop away and disappear, taking with them time and space. You rest in silence.

Write what you have experienced.

Find your silence, close your eyes and rest. Allow an unknown colored shape to appear, one for which you have no label. Let this spontaneous blob of color do its own thing. Let it change in size, shape, in near or far spatial position. Let it envelop you if it wishes, filling your body with color. Let the color drip out of your eyes, your ears, your mouth, out through your fingers and toes. When it wishes, let the shape suck the color back into itself.

Let it change into another color as you observe. Allow it to change into as many different colors as it feels is interesting. Let a strain of music accompany the movements of the colored shapes. Notice if the music changes as the colors change. Do the shapes and colors follow the music, or does the music follow their lead? Continue observing this dance of the forms, color, space, and music until they spontaneously exit of their own accord, leaving the stage of your mind to its own imageless silence.

Write your experiences.

Find your silence, close your eyes and rest in
this dynamic silence. Visualize walking through
a murky, steaming swamp of decaying animal
and vegetable matter, overhung with dense
vines and trees. Let the acrid, loathsome odors
engulf you. Feel the hideous slime under
your bare feet, oozing through your toes as
each foot is sucked and held in an iron hand
as you tortuously struggle forward. Feel yourself fighting the swarms of insects that threat-
en to engulf you. As you inch your way
through endless time, you catch a faint glim-
mer of light in the far distance, and tortuously make your way toward it — step by
agonizing step. Suddenly the light grows
brighter, and then, as if your body melted
through a transparent wall of luminous radiance, the swamp vanishes, and you find yourself in a garden of indescribable beauty. It is
filled with all of the flowers you have ever
known and loved; the air is ladened with their
rich fragrance. You are aware of music com-
ing from nowhere and everywhere, so perfect
and sublime, it will haunt you the rest of your
life. As you stand in wonder, filling all of
your senses with this beauty, you notice a
rocky grotto, at the farthest corner of the garden, carved from magnificent precious stones
of dazzling color and description. As you walk
into the grotto you behold a fountain of spar-
kling, dancing water which you realize, as you
draw near it, is not water, but a scintillating,
spiraling column of light, reaching to the
vaulted ceiling of the grotto. In rapturous de-
light you step into the column and find yourself spiraling and dancing, winging through
space with the light, in an exalted, disembodied

Day 5

ectasy, released from time and space. You continue to bathe in the light, dancing with the music, filled with the fragrance of the flowers, until the music fades, the fragrance drifts away, and the light vanishes. You are standing in deep, velvety silence, but left with an undefinable sense of calm, aware of the universe opening before you as a unified and integrated whole.

When you return to earth, write all of your experiences.

On this day, choose any previous day that you found most helpful in experiencing the silence, and repeat it. Write what you found new this time compared with the first day you worked with it.

Summary

In this book nothing is taught *about* visualization, only an invitation is given to you, the reader and student, to learn by doing. Only through doing and writing can you learn about your own inner process of visualization. Merely reading the projects is no substitute for working with them, and writing your experiences.

Through practicing the visual skills and principles presented, you have the opportunity of finding untapped creative resources within yourself, of developing skills carrying far wider application, of discovering this learning, living within you, and becoming part of your life. With your senses attuned to a different rhythm, responding to a new sense of frequency, you can experience a flowing time-space unity.

Disruptive events will always occur in your days to lure you from harmony and unity, but as you continue practicing the projects, making them part of daily living, the disorders will change into valuable learning experiences. Problems will become opportunities. Each here and now moment in time can be valued as a gift from thousands of past moments of discovery. They are gifts to be welcomed rather than ignored, accepted rather than rejected, gifts to be identified, encouraged and appreciated.

As visual learning and thinking become part of your living, you can realize more and more profoundly the power of visualization. As you abide in the NOW, letting the silence of visualization direct you, there will be answers in the NOW for all days. Time-space will be perceived as one total structure in a flash of recognition.

CLOSING STATEMENT

This moment is all we have
  Dear Ones
Whether in moonlight or darkness
  or sun
Hold it tenderly — then —
  let it go
Make room for the next
  so we may grow
The past is part of it
The future is too
But — this moment
  is living
For me —
  and for you

References

1. Adams, James L., Conceptual Blockbusting. W. H. Freeman & Co. 1974
2. Bangs, Helen. Mind Psi Biotics Seminar. San Diego, Ca. February 1976
3. Blair, Lawrence. Rhythms of Vision. Shocken Books 1976
4. Brunton, Paul. The Secret Path. E. P. Dutton & Co. 1935
5. Capra, Fritjof. The Tao of Physics. Shambhala Publications 1975
6. De Bono, Edward. Lateral Thinking. Harper & Row 1970
7. Fitch, Herbert. Kauai, Hawaii, Infinite Way Seminar, April 1978
8. Fitch, Herbert. Avila Beach, California. Infinite Way Seminar, October 1979
9. Forrest, Elliott. Vision and the Language Arts. Optical Journal Review, Jan. 1967
10. Getman, G. N. Otter Crest Seminar, Oregon, September 1976
11. Goldsmith, Joel. All Infinite Way publications from 1947 through 1964. Available through DeVorss & Co., Santa Monica, Ca.
12. Hamel, Peter Michael. Through Music to the Self. Shambhala 1979
13. Huxley, Aldous. Island. Harper & Row 1962
14. Karagulla, Shafica. Breakthrough to Creativity. DeVorss & Co. 1967

15. Leonard, George. The Silent Pulse. E. P. Dutton 1978
16. Lyons, C. V. & Emily B. The Power of Visual Training as Measured in Factors of Intelligence. Journal of the American Optometric Assn. December 1954. Reprinted by Optometric Extension Program Foundation. Duncan, Oklahoma
17. Lyons, C. V. & Emily B. The Power of Visual Training II. Further Case Studies measured in Factors of Intelligence. Journal of the AOA. November 1956. Reprinted by OEPF, Duncan, Oklahoma
18. Lyons, C. V. & Emily B. The Power of Optometric Visual Training III: A Loom for Productive Thinking. Journal of the AOA, June 1957. Reprinted by OEPF, Duncan, Oklahoma
19. Lyons, C. V. & Emily B. The Power of Optometric Visual Training IV: To Build Minds. Journal of the AOA, June 1961. Reprinted by OEPF, Duncan, Oklahoma
20. Lyons, C. V. & Emily B. The Power of Optometric Visual Training V: Explored Through a Philosophy of Visualization. Journal of the AOA, August 1967. Reprinted by OEPF, Duncan, Ok.
21. Lyons, C. V. & Emily B. A Search Model for Optometry. Transcript West Coast Visual Training Conference, San Jose, Ca. 1957
22. Lyons, C. V. & Emily B. Visual Signs: Cuing Agents to Productive Thinking. Transcript West Coast Visual Training Conference, San Jose, Ca. 1958
23. Lyons, C. V. & Emily B. Visualization Series: Units I, II, IV, V. Golden Rule Publications, Willits, Ca.
24. Lyons, C. V. & Emily B. Visualization Series Unit III: Visual Signs: The Principles of Abstraction and Visualization. Golden Rule Publications, Willits, Ca.
25. Lyons, C. V. & Emily B. Relating Body Awareness and Effortless Motion to Visual Training. Published in: Teaching Through Sensory-Motor Experiences, Academic Therapy Publications 1969. Edited by John Arena
26. Maslow, Abraham. Religions, Values and Peak Experiences. Viking Press 1970
27. Ornstein, Robert E. Psychology of Consciousness. W. H. Freeman & Co. 1972
28. Osburn, Alex F. Applied Imagination. Charles Scribner's Sons 1963

29. Ott, John N. Health and Light. Simon & Schuster 1973

30. Oyle, Irving. The Healing Mind. Celestial Arts 1975

31. Patten, Bernard M. Visually Mediated Thinking: A Report of the Case of Albert Einstein. Journal of Learning Disabilities, August 1973

32. Perls, F.; Hefferline, R.; Goodman, P. Gestalt Therapy. Julian Press 1962

33. Samuels, M. and Samuels, N. Seeing with the Mind's Eye. Random House 1975

34. Stearn, Jess. The Power of Alpha Thinking. Signet Books 1977